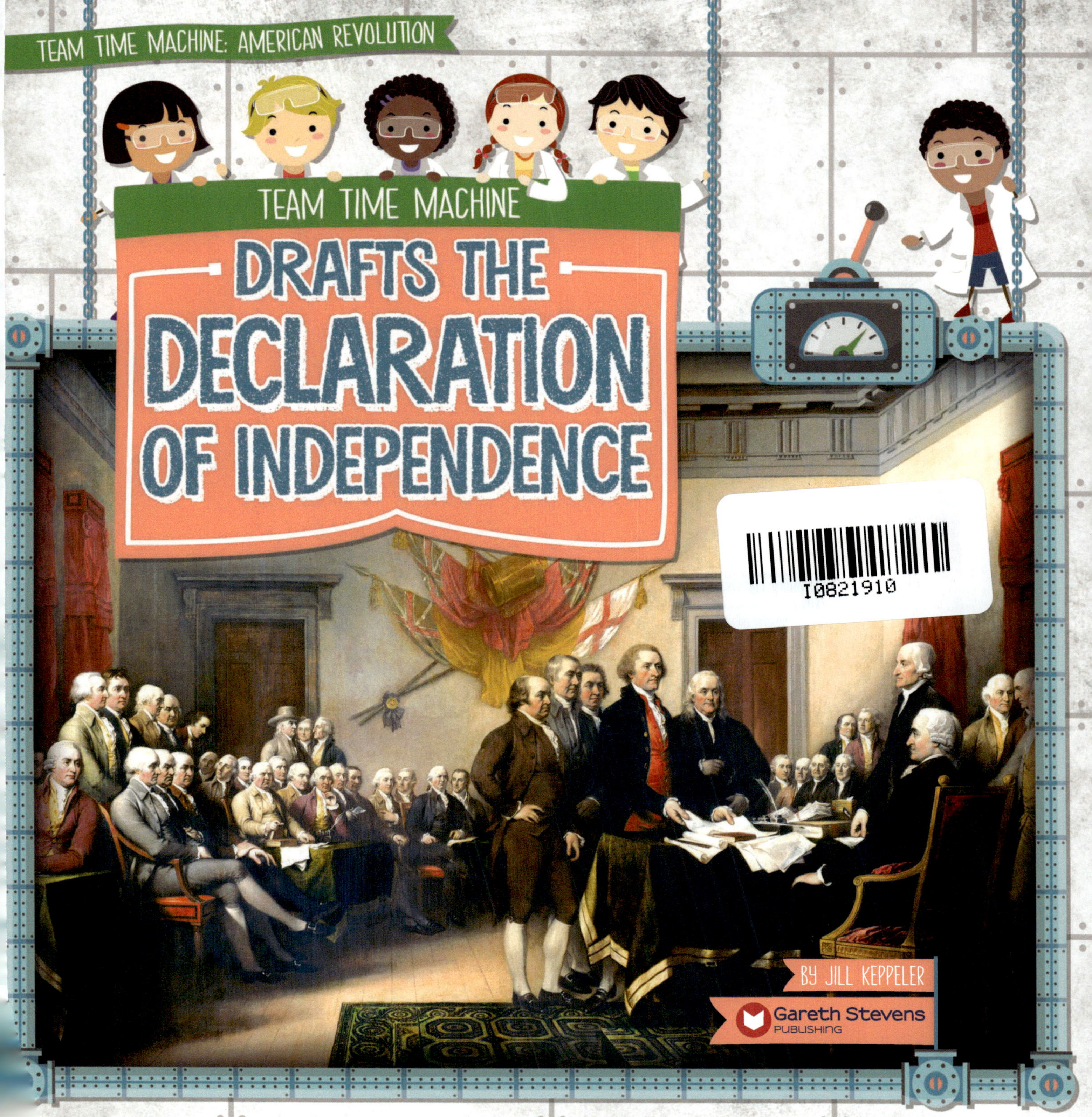
TEAM TIME MACHINE: AMERICAN REVOLUTION
TEAM TIME MACHINE
DRAFTS THE
DECLARATION
OF INDEPENDENCE
BY JILL KEPPELER
Gareth Stevens
PUBLISHING

Please visit our website, www.garethstevens.com. For a free color catalog of all our high-quality books, call toll free 1-800-542-2595 or fax 1-877-542-2596.

Library of Congress Cataloging-in-Publication Data

Names: Keppeler, Jill, author.
Title: Team time machine drafts the Declaration of Independence / Jill Keppeler.
Description: New York : Gareth Stevens Publishing, [2020] | Series: Team time machine: American Revolution | Includes bibliographical references and index.
Identifiers: LCCN 2019013918| ISBN 9781538246788 (pbk.) | ISBN 9781538246801 (library bound) | ISBN 9781538246795 (6 pack)
Subjects: LCSH: United States. Declaration of Independence–Juvenile literature. | United States–History–Revolution, 1775-1783–Juvenile literature.
Classification: LCC E221 .K46 2020 | DDC 973.3/13–dc23
LC record available at https://lccn.loc.gov/2019013918

First Edition

Published in 2020 by
Gareth Stevens Publishing
111 East 14th Street, Suite 349
New York, NY 10003

Designer: Katelyn E. Reynolds
Editor: Therese Shea

Photo credits: Cover, pp. 1, 23 GraphicaArtis/Getty Images; cover, pp. 1–24 (series characters) Lorelyn Medina/Shutterstock.com; cover, pp. 1–24 (time machine elements) Agor2012/Shutterstock.com; cover, pp. 1–24 (background texture) somen/Shutterstock.com; p. 5 Todd Taulman Photography/Shutterstock.com; p. 7 Thiranun Kunatum/Shutterstock.com; p. 9 (main) Fernando Garcia Esteban/Shutterstock.com; p. 9 (map) Weredragon/Shutterstock.com; p. 11 Sean Pavone/Shutterstock.com; p. 12 (nickel) Jessica R. McNair/Shutterstock.com; p. 13 Steve Lovegrove/Shutterstock.com; p. 14 Smith Collection/Gado/Archive Photos/Getty Images; p. 15 Beyond My Ken/Wikipedia.org; p. 17 Courtesy of the National Museum of American History, Smithsonian Institution/Library of Congress; p. 19 Douglas Graham/CQ-Roll Call Group/Getty Images; pp. 21, 27 (main) Universal History Archive/Getty Images; p. 25 Hulton Archive/Getty Images.

Printed in the United States of America

CPSIA compliance information: Batch #CW20GS: For further information contact Gareth Stevens, New York, New York at 1-800-542-2595.

CONTENTS

WORDS IN THE GLOSSARY APPEAR IN **BOLD** TYPE THE FIRST TIME THEY ARE USED IN THE TEXT.

CHAPTER 1: FIRST DRAFTS

"Ugh!" Ben said as he walked down the school hall with Mia and Sam.

He looked down at the paper in his hands. "Mrs. Bennett marked up my English paper a lot. I thought I did a good job!"

"It's a first **draft**, right?" Mia asked. "You're supposed to have it marked up and then make it better."

Sam nodded. "Mrs. Bennett says editing happens to everyone who is a writer. Even Thomas Jefferson! And he wrote the **Declaration of Independence**!"

MEET TEAM TIME MACHINE

TEAM TIME MACHINE IS A GROUP OF FRIENDS WHO FOUND A TIME MACHINE IN A VERY ODD LIBRARY. THEY DISCOVERED THAT BOOKS FROM THE LIBRARY COULD POWER THE MACHINE AND TRANSPORT THEM TO DIFFERENT PLACES AND TIMES. IN THIS ADVENTURE, MIA, BEN, AND SAM MEET THOMAS JEFFERSON!

THE DECLARATION OF INDEPENDENCE IS ONE OF THE MOST FAMOUS AND IMPORTANT PIECES OF WRITING IN AMERICAN HISTORY.

"That doesn't mean I like editing!" Ben said.

"Nobody does!" Sam laughed. "I bet all writers feel that way."

Mia agreed. "I bet even Thomas Jefferson didn't like editing!"

Ben cheered up. "We're studying Jefferson and the Declaration of Independence in social studies," he said. "Let's go to the Team Time Machine library and visit him! We can learn more about the Declaration *and* about Thomas Jefferson."

"Great idea!" said Sam and Mia.

THIS IS THE TEAM TIME MACHINE LIBRARY. TO VISIT ANY PLACE AND TIME, ALL YOU NEED TO DO IS PLACE A BOOK IN THE TIME MACHINE AND PULL THE HANDLE!

CHAPTER 2: OFF TO PHILLY

It didn't take the team long to find a book called *The Writing of the Declaration of Independence*. There was a picture of Thomas Jefferson on the cover.

"Here we go!" Ben said. He placed it in the machine. The room started to shake. The kids tried to steady themselves as the room spun. After a few moments, the shaking stopped.

Sam bounced to his feet and ran to the door. The others followed. They peered outside. They could see the streets of Philadelphia, Pennsylvania—in 1776!

BY JULY 1776, THE **AMERICAN REVOLUTION** HAD ALREADY BEEN FOUGHT FOR MORE THAN A YEAR. IT HAD STARTED WITH THE BATTLES OF LEXINGTON AND CONCORD ON APRIL 19, 1775.

BY THE 1770S, ABOUT 30,000 PEOPLE LIVED IN PHILADELPHIA, INCLUDING BENJAMIN FRANKLIN. SOME HISTORIC PLACES CAN BE VISITED AT FRANKLIN COURT, SHOWN HERE.

CHAPTER 3: A VERY IMPORTANT EVENT

The kids decided to find the house where Thomas Jefferson was staying. They started walking through the streets of Philadelphia, looking around with great interest. None of the colonists seemed to know there was an important event happening!

The team knew that the Second **Continental Congress** was meeting in the Pennsylvania State House in Philadelphia. That group of leaders had given five men the duty of drafting a declaration, or official statement, of independence. This "**Committee** of Five" picked Jefferson to do most of the writing.

THE CONTINENTAL CONGRESS PICKED THE COMMITTEE OF FIVE, WHICH INCLUDED THOMAS JEFFERSON, JOHN ADAMS, BENJAMIN FRANKLIN, ROGER SHERMAN, AND ROBERT LIVINGSTON.

THE PENNSYLVANIA STATE HOUSE STILL STANDS TODAY. IT'S NOW CALLED INDEPENDENCE HALL.

CHAPTER 4: FINDING THOMAS

Philadelphia was a big city, even in 1776. The kids realized finding Jefferson's house might be harder than they thought. They stopped to figure out what to do. Maybe they could go to the State House and look for him there?

Then, Ben looked down the street. He pointed at a man walking toward them. He was tall and had reddish hair. Mia pulled a nickel out of her pocket. The man looked a lot like the picture of Jefferson on the nickel!

JEFFERSON BECAME THE FACE ON THE US NICKEL IN 1938. THERE ARE DIFFERENT KINDS OF JEFFERSON NICKELS, HOWEVER.

The friends followed Jefferson down the street. He stopped at a big house made of red bricks at the corner of two streets. Then he went inside. Mia, Ben, and Sam looked at each other. After a minute, Sam went up to the door. He knocked.

A boy about their age opened the door. He said his name was James. He worked for Jacob Graff Jr., who owned the house. "We're here to see Mr. Jefferson," Ben told him.

WHILE HE WAS IN PHILADELPHIA, JEFFERSON RENTED ROOMS IN A BIG BRICK HOUSE NOW CALLED THE GRAFF HOUSE OR THE DECLARATION HOUSE. YOU CAN VISIT A RE-CREATION OF HOW THE HOUSE LOOKED BACK THEN.

CHAPTER 5: MEETING THE MAN

"Before I take you to Mr. Jefferson, what are you wearing?" James asked. The team realized they looked very odd in their clothes from the future!

"These are our traveling clothes! We're not from around here," Sam explained quickly.

James nodded and asked them to follow him. All four kids walked up the stairs. James knocked on the door. A voice inside told them to come in. Mia pushed the door open. Thomas Jefferson was sitting at a table.

THOMAS JEFFERSON WAS A GOOD WRITER. HE ALSO LOVED BOOKS. HE LATER SOLD HIS LIBRARY OF 6,500 BOOKS TO THE LIBRARY OF CONGRESS.

THOMAS JEFFERSON WROTE THE DECLARATION ON A SMALL, MOVABLE DESK, OR "WRITING BOX," OF HIS OWN CREATION.

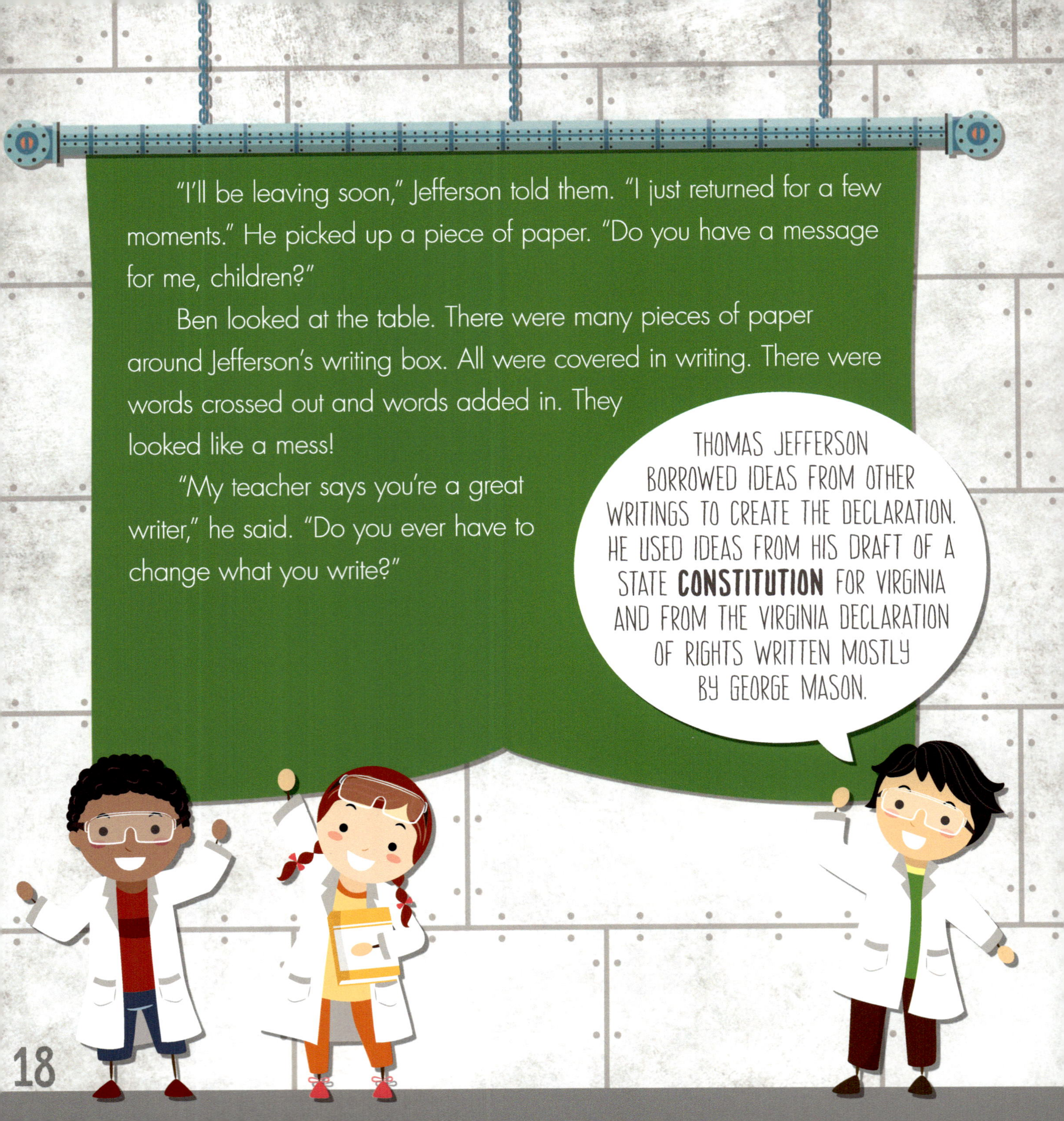

"I'll be leaving soon," Jefferson told them. "I just returned for a few moments." He picked up a piece of paper. "Do you have a message for me, children?"

Ben looked at the table. There were many pieces of paper around Jefferson's writing box. All were covered in writing. There were words crossed out and words added in. They looked like a mess!

"My teacher says you're a great writer," he said. "Do you ever have to change what you write?"

DRAFTS OF THE DECLARATION OF INDEPENDENCE SHOW WHERE JEFFERSON CROSSED OUT AND ADDED WORDS.

CHAPTER 6: DONE BY COMMITTEE

Jefferson laughed. "Yes," he told Ben. "I change my writing until I'm satisfied." He turned toward the door. "Follow me."

The kids followed Jefferson down the street. He told them that he was carrying his "fair copy" of the Declaration of Independence. He'd made a new copy after Benjamin Franklin and John Adams, two of the other members of the Committee of Five, made changes to the original. Then, the full committee **approved** it. Now, he was taking it to the whole Continental Congress!

JOHN ADAMS TALKED JEFFERSON INTO WRITING THE DRAFT. HE LATER SAID THAT HE TOLD JEFFERSON, "YOU CAN WRITE TEN TIMES BETTER THAN I CAN."

THIS PICTURE SHOWS FRANKLIN (LEFT) AND ADAMS (MIDDLE) LOOKING OVER A DRAFT OF THE DECLARATION OF INDEPENDENCE WITH JEFFERSON.

CHAPTER 7: PRESENTING THE DRAFT

The kids followed Jefferson to the Pennsylvania State House. He went to a big room that was crowded with people. Mia, Sam, and Ben slipped into the back and watched. Jefferson joined four other men, and they walked to the front. The crowd hushed as they presented the declaration. A man started reading the **document** out loud.

"It sounds a little different from what I remember," Ben whispered to the others, who nodded. Still, it started the same way.

ON JULY 2, THE CONTINENTAL CONGRESS APPROVED THE **RESOLUTION** TO DECLARE INDEPENDENCE. BUT THEY DIDN'T APPROVE THE DOCUMENT CALLED THE DECLARATION OF INDEPENDENCE UNTIL 2 DAYS LATER.

THE SECOND CONTINENTAL CONGRESS RETURNED TO THE STATE HOUSE ON JULY 1, 1776—AND THEN THEY STARTING **DEBATING** PARTS OF THE DECLARATION OF INDEPENDENCE.

CHAPTER 8: ARGUING AND EDITING

The team stuck around for a few days. They stayed with their new friend James and explored Philadelphia. And when the Continental Congress met again, they were in the back again, watching.

Wow, could those **delegates** argue! And they edited, too. They took out parts of Jefferson's declaration and changed others.

"Jefferson doesn't look happy," Mia whispered, pointing to the writer. It looked like Benjamin Franklin was trying to cheer him up.

"No, he doesn't!" Ben agreed.

JEFFERSON REALLY WASN'T HAPPY! BENJAMIN FRANKLIN AND OTHER FRIENDS TRIED TO MAKE HIM FEEL BETTER ABOUT THE CHANGES. ADAMS LATER SAID THAT THE CONTINENTAL CONGRESS "**OBLITERATED** SOME OF THE BEST OF IT."

THE OTHER MEMBERS OF THE SECOND CONTINENTAL CONGRESS TOOK OUT ABOUT ONE-FOURTH OF JEFFERSON'S WORDS IN THE DECLARATION OF INDEPENDENCE.

Finally, it was July 4, 1776. The delegates kept arguing and changing the Declaration right up through the morning! But then it was time—the group settled down to take a vote on the declaration. The friends knew what was coming, but they still cheered when it was approved.

Jefferson still didn't look entirely happy, but he smiled at them as the kids slipped out the door and headed for the library. "We just saw the first Independence Day!" Mia said. "Wow!"

MOST OF THE PEOPLE WHO SIGNED THE DECLARATION OF INDEPENDENCE DID IT ON AUGUST 2, 1776. A FEW DELEGATES SIGNED IT LATER. JOHN HANCOCK, THE PRESIDENT OF THE CONGRESS, WAS THE FIRST PERSON TO SIGN IT.

THIS PRINT SHOWS MEMBERS OF THE SECOND CONTINENTAL CONGRESS LEAVING THE PENNSYLVANIA STATE HOUSE AFTER ADOPTING THE DECLARATION OF INDEPENDENCE.

CHAPTER 10: WE HOLD THESE TRUTHS

Back in their own time, Ben said, "It's okay if Mrs. Bennett gives me suggestions for my writing. The Declaration of Independence was changed a lot, so I guess my papers can be, too!"

"It took many people—and many suggestions—to create the United States we know today," Sam said.

As they went to social studies class, Team Time Machine said Jefferson's words together, "We hold these truths to be **self-evident**, that all men are created equal . . . "

IN CLASS, WE WORKED ON THE TIMELINE OF THE DECLARATION OF INDEPENDENCE ON THE NEXT PAGE. WE WERE THERE FOR MANY OF THESE DATES!

TIMELINE

THE SECOND CONTINENTAL CONGRESS FIRST MEETS.	MAY 10, 1775	
	JUNE 7, 1776	DELEGATE RICHARD HENRY LEE ASKS THE CONGRESS TO DECLARE INDEPENDENCE FROM ENGLAND.
THE CONGRESS APPOINTS THE COMMITTEE OF FIVE, INCLUDING THOMAS JEFFERSON, TO DRAFT AN OFFICIAL DECLARATION OF INDEPENDENCE.	JUNE 11, 1776	
	JUNE 28, 1776	THE COMMITTEE PRESENTS THE DRAFT OF THE DECLARATION OF INDEPENDENCE TO THE CONTINENTAL CONGRESS.
THE CONGRESS DEBATES AND CHANGES PARTS OF THE DECLARATION OF INDEPENDENCE.	JULY 1 TO 4, 1776	
	JULY 2, 1776	THE CONGRESS APPROVES LEE'S RESOLUTION, DECLARING INDEPENDENCE.
THE CONGRESS ADOPTS THE DECLARATION OF INDEPENDENCE.	JULY 4, 1776	
	AUGUST 2, 1776	MOST OF THE DELEGATES SIGN THE DECLARATION OF INDEPENDENCE.

GLOSSARY

American Revolution: the war in which the colonies won their freedom from England

approve: to give official agreement

committee: a group of people chosen to do a certain job

constitution: the basic laws by which a country or state is governed

Continental Congress: a meeting of colonial representatives before, during, and after the American Revolution

debate: to have a public discussion or argument

Declaration of Independence: the piece of writing in which the colonies said they were free from British rule

delegate: a representative of one of the 13 colonies

document: a formal or official piece of writing

draft: a document before completion. Also, to put something into written form.

obliterate: to completely destroy

resolution: an official statement of purpose voted on by a group

self-evident: clearly true

FOR MORE INFORMATION

BOOKS

Harris, Michael C. *What Is the Declaration of Independence?* New York, NY: Grosset & Dunlap, 2016.

Maloof, Torrey. *Thomas Jefferson and the Empire of Liberty.* Huntington Beach, CA: Teacher Created Materials, 2017.

Morlock, Jeremy. *Problem-Solving Methods of the Continental Congress.* New York, NY: PowerKids Press, 2019.

WEBSITES

BrainPop: Thomas Jefferson
www.brainpop.com/socialstudies/famoushistoricalfigures/thomasjefferson/
How much do you really know about the Founding Father and third president of the United States?

Declaration of Independence: 1776
bensguide.gpo.gov/declaration-of-independence-1776
Learn more about the background of this important US document.

National Geographic Kids: Independence Day
kids.nationalgeographic.com/explore/history/independence-day/
There's more to this holiday than fireworks and parades.

Publisher's note to educators and parents: Our editors have carefully reviewed these websites to ensure that they are suitable for students. Many websites change frequently, however, and we cannot guarantee that a site's future contents will continue to meet our high standards of quality and educational value. Be advised that students should be closely supervised whenever they access the internet.

INDEX